GUIDE TO

ISRAEL

September 1995

DAVID MARSHALL

Highlights for Children

CONTENTS

On the cover: The 1,300-year-old Dome of the Rock mosque in Jerusalem, built by Muslims on the site of the ancient Jewish Temple

Published by Highlights for Children
© 1996 Highlights for Children, Inc.
P.O. Box 18201
Columbus, Ohio 43218-0201

10 9 8 7 6 5 4 3 2
ISBN 0-87534-923-4

EUROPE

Israel

ASIA

AFRICA

AUSTRALIA

ANTARCTICA

△ **Israel's flag** Blue stripes on white represent the cloth of a *tallit*, a prayer shawl worn by religious Jews. The six-pointed star symbolizes the unity of the Jewish people. It is commonly known as the Star of David. David was the second king of ancient Israel.

ISRAEL AT A GLANCE

Area 7,992 square miles (20,780 square kilometers)

Population 5 million

Capital Jerusalem (population 524,000)

Other big cities Tel Aviv (population of city and metropolitan districts almost 2 million), Haifa (245,900)

Highest mountain Mt. Meron, 3,985 feet (1,208 meters)

Longest river Jordan, 120 miles (192 kilometers)

Largest lake Sea of Galilee, 64 square miles (166 square kilometers)

Official languages Hebrew, Arabic

▷ **Israeli money** Israel's currency is the *shekel*. On the 10-shekel note is a picture of Golda Meir, Israel's Prime Minister from 1969 to 1974.

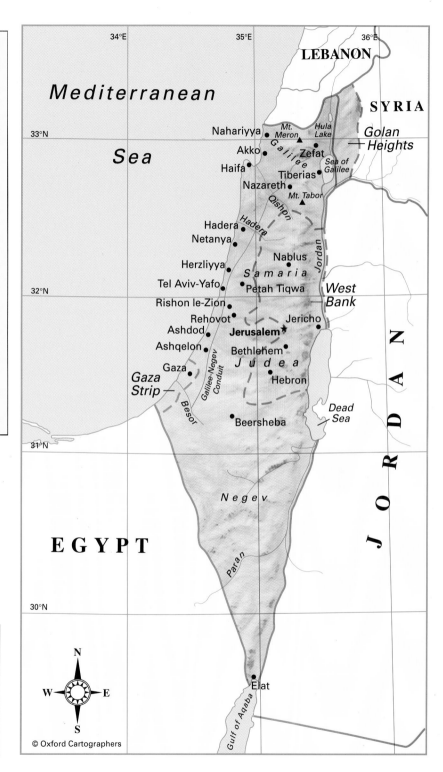

◁ **Israeli stamps** Two of the stamps shown here feature historical pictures of some transportation services. The others show views of plant and animal wildlife in Israel.

Map current as of December 1995. Place names in Israel have a long history so are denoted in a variety of ways, for example, Yafo and Jaffa; Hefa and Haifa; Eilat and Elat; and Be'er Sheva and Beersheba. The Gulf of Elat, an arm of the Red Sea, is also called the Gulf of Aqaba.

ISRAEL

Desert	★ Capital
Farmland	● Major Cities
	▲ Mountain Peaks
	— Country Boundary
	– – Other Territories

0   10   20   30 Miles
0   20   40 Kilometers

Map labels

LEBANON
SYRIA
Mediterranean
Sea
33°N
Nahariyya
Mt. Meron
Hula Lake
Golan Heights
Akko
Zefat
Galilee
Sea of Galilee
Haifa
Tiberias
Nazareth
Mt. Tabor
Qishon
Hadera
Hadera
Netanya
Nablus
Herzliyya
Samaria
Jordan
Tel Aviv-Yafo
Petah Tiqwa
West Bank
32°N
Rishon le-Zion
Rehovot
Jericho
Ashdod
Jerusalem ★
Ashqelon
Bethlehem
Gaza
Judea
Hebron
Gaza Strip
Galilee-Negev Conduit
Dead Sea
Besor
Beersheba
JORDAN
31°N
Negev
EGYPT
Paran
30°N
N
W   E
S
© Oxford Cartographers
Elat
Gulf of Aqaba
34°E   35°E   36°E

5

WELCOME TO ISRAEL

Israel is a small country at the southeastern end of the Mediterranean Sea. In less than seven hours you can travel by bus from Elat in the south to Haifa in the north, passing through Israel's biggest city, Tel Aviv, on the Mediterranean coast. In ancient times, this area was called Canaan. The "modern" nation of Israel was founded in 1948.

Israel has varied scenery. In the south is the barren Negev, a desertlike region, where few people live. The coastal plains in the west are good farmland. Away from the sea there are mountains, valleys, lakes, and rivers. The climate is mostly dry, but more rain falls in the north than in the south. The Jordan River flows southward through the Sea of Galilee to the Dead Sea and supplies much of Israel's water.

Israel is a Jewish state with a large minority of Arabs. Most of the Jewish people belong to smaller groups — the Sephardic Jews, who came from Spain in the 1400s, and the Ashkenazic, who arrived from Germany and Eastern Europe in the 20th century. People are still arriving from Europe, Russia, and North America to live in Israel.

The modern world mixes with the ancient in Israel. Israel is a leading producer of hospital equipment and computers, and its people have turned some desert land into fruit orchards. Side by side with the modern buildings are the ancient sites of Jerusalem, the Dead Sea, and many other places known from the Bible.

Modern Israel has had conflicts with its neighboring countries, but lately they have made peace, one by one. The hope is to bring lasting peace to this fascinating and beautiful country and to the whole area of the Middle East.

▷ **A street market near the Damascus Gate** The gate marks the start of the ancient road that once led from Jerusalem to Damascus in Syria.

◁ **Olive terraces** Some of the oldest olive trees in the world can be found in Israel. They may be more than 2,000 years old.

▽ **The Basilica of the Annunciation** Built in the 1970s, this church stands on the site where many believe the Virgin Mary was told that she would give birth to Jesus.

THE GOLDEN OLD CITY

Jerusalem is the capital city of Israel with a population of 524,000. It has old and new areas. The Old City is a holy place for Jews, Christians, and Muslims. It is filled with sites that are important to people of each faith. Both Judaism and Christianity — two of the three religions that believe in only one god — started in Israel. And the third, Islam, gained its inspiration from them. Also, the Holy Bible, including the Old and New Testaments, were written in this land.

King Solomon, who lived between 970 and 928 B.C., built a Temple for Israel. It was ruined in 586 B.C. by the Babylonians. The second Temple, built in 521 B.C., was made bigger by King Herod in 20 B.C. This Temple was destroyed by the Romans in A.D. 70. Its only remaining part is the Western Wall, so this is the most sacred place for all Jews. Religious Jews come here to pray and to mourn the loss of the Temple and the destruction of ancient Jerusalem. Hence, the Wall is also named "the Wailing Wall."

The Dome of the Rock mosque was built on the ruins of the Jewish Temple between A.D. 688 and 691. The rock marks the prophet Mohammed's journey to heaven on horseback. This is a holy place for all Muslims, who believe that a footprint and some hairs from Mohammed's beard have been preserved here.

The churches and gardens on the Mount of Olives, in the Old City, mark the last days in the life of Jesus. The Garden of Gethsemane is said to be the place where Roman soldiers arrested Jesus. (The Romans ruled the country at the time.) The Via Dolorosa follows the last journey Jesus made, and the Church of the Holy Sepulcher is built on the place where he died.

▽ **The Western Wall** The Old City wall was built around 50 B.C. to hold up the western side of the Jewish Temple. The Dome of the Rock can be seen in the background.

◁ **Rooftops and courtyards** This aerial view shows the Jewish section of the Old City of Jerusalem.

Sunset over Jerusalem On the right are the golden domes of the Church of Maria Magdalena, and in the center is the ancient town wall.

CAPITAL OF CONTRASTS

Jerusalem's Old City is famous for its busy street markets. Many local people shop on Suq Khan ez-Zeit Street, which runs from Damascus Gate to the center of the Old City. There are stalls on nearby El-Wad Street and along David Street. Here there are specialty markets such as the Butcher's Market and the Clothier's Market. There is a modern shopping mall nearby at the Cardo.

The New City is like most capital cities today. There are many apartment buildings, government offices, and museums. Notice that all homes in the city are covered with Jerusalem stone from nearby quarries.

One of the most important sights in the New City is the Yad Vashem Memorial. This was built for all the Jews who were killed during the Holocaust, which took place between 1939 and 1945. Two million names of the six million who died are recorded here. A flame burns in their memory and is never allowed to go out.

▽ **The Bronze Menorah** This symbolic (candle) lamp honors the State of Israel.

▽ **Orthodox Jews at their religious studies** Their college is called a *yeshiva.*

In the western part of the New City is Israel's parliament building, the *Knesset*. At certain times you can go inside to see the legislature at work. Nearby, at the Hebrew University, you can see the National House of Books, which includes a collection of all books printed in Israel.

▽ **Modern Jerusalem** In the foreground are the roofs of the Israel Museum. The square building on the left is the Knesset.

SHEPHERDS IN THE HILLS

As you leave Jerusalem traveling along the Jericho-to-Jerusalem Highway, you will see the hills of Samaria and Judaea. These hills have always been popular with nomads. These people move from place to place seeking new land to feed their animals. The towns of Bethlehem, Hebron, and Nablus lie in the hills a little further south.

The town of Bethlehem is important to all Christians. It is said that Jesus Christ was born here. A church has been built over the site. It is called the Church of the Nativity. Inside, in the Grotto of the Nativity, a small, bright, silver star shape is set in the ground. Much of the decoration in the church has faded, but this star still shines. Nearby is the Milk Grotto Chapel. It is said that while nursing Jesus here, Mary spilled some milk onto the stone floor. The building has remained milky white ever since.

Like many buildings in Israel, Rachel's Tomb, to the north of the center of Bethlehem, is holy to Jews and also to Christians and Muslims. Rachel, one of the wives of Jacob and mother of Joseph and Benjamin, is a much-loved figure in the Old Testament of the Bible. Her tomb is a very popular place of worship, especially for women.

To the southeast of Bethlehem is the hill where you will find the remains of Herod the Great's summer palace. Herod built his summer palace between 24 and 15 B.C. In the summer palace there was once a white marble stairway leading to the towers, the bathrooms, and Herod's own vast rooms. Most of the building was destroyed in a war between Romans and Jews in A.D. 132 to 135.

This palace overlooks the ancient biblical town of Hebron, where a fascinating Arab market is held. You can buy traditional clothes, craftworks, and local dishes ranging from peaches in syrup to camel meat. There are some fine examples of Egyptian-style architecture around the market.

▷ **Nomad tent near Bethlehem** The Bedouins are nomads who settle for a while with their herds and then move on. The rolling hills outside Bethlehem are good pasture for the animals. And the nomads have enough space to pitch their tents.

▽ **The town of Nablus** Today this town is the capital of the region of Samaria, but it is full of biblical history. Jacob pitched a tent here, and Jesus is said to have drawn water from the well.

12

▽ **The Herodian** Herod's magnificent summer palace was destroyed in the first century A.D. Byzantine monks from Turkey later set up a monastery in the ruins.

13

JERICHO AND THE DEAD SEA

The history of the city of Jericho stretches back as far as 8000 B.C. Scientists studying the past have discovered that it was here that the world's very first farming settlements grew up. In the nearby desert, the land and the weather are poor for farming, but in Jericho conditions are good. Today, the farmers of Jericho produce lots of fruit and flowers for the colorful local markets.

The Jordan River to the east of Jericho stretches for 120 miles (192 kilometers) and is Israel's longest river. Its springs and streams are the major source of drinking water in the country. The Jordan River flows southward to the Dead Sea from the Sea of Galilee. The Dead Sea is 1,320 feet (400 meters) below sea level, the world's lowest land elevation. Water in the Dead Sea is the saltiest on earth and will hold you up even if you cannot swim. Qumran, on the northwest shore of the sea, is where the famous Dead Sea Scrolls were found stored in earthenware jars. They tell what life was like in the first century A.D. The scrolls were discovered in a cave by a Bedouin shepherd in 1947.

Herod the Great's fabulous fortress at Masada was built on a mountain overlooking the Dead Sea. It was used for more than defense. The luxurious living quarters included grand public baths. The rooms, all decorated in different styles, were supplied with water from twelve tanks.

The West Bank area is not officially part of the State of Israel, and Arab zones within it are now gaining the rights of self-government. From here, one can enter the country of Jordan by way of the Allenby Bridge.

▷ **The ruins of the Fortress of Masada** Masada is a symbol of the heroic last battle of Jewish warriors against the conquering Roman army in A.D. 73.

◁ Floating in the Dead Sea

The salt in the water keeps swimmers afloat. The sea and its minerals are famous for health benefits.

▽ Synagogue at Masada

This is among the oldest and best preserved synagogues, or Jewish place of worship, in the world.

THE NORTH

The Lower and Upper Galilee are the northern regions of Israel, with the Golan Heights to their East. The Galilee was the the main political and spiritual Jewish center from about 300 B.C. to A.D. 600. Many Christian miracles are said to have taken place here in Jesus's time.

Israel's climate and scenery are varied in this area. In winter, people can sunbathe on the shores of the Sea of Galilee and then go skiing at Mount Hermon, a small resort at the far northern tip of the country.

▽ **Fishermen selling their catch at Tiberias**
Fishing in the Sea of Galilee is a typical local occupation with a long tradition.

The Sea of Galilee is really a large freshwater lake, not a sea. The Israelis call it by its ancient name, Lake Kinneret. Water is piped from the lake to many parts of Israel where little rain falls. The Israelis also make good use of the sun, another major natural resource for the country. Many homes are built with solar panels on the roof. They use the year-round sunshine to heat their water.

In the Galilee and the Golan regions you can also visit Druze villages. The Druze are a small minority of Israeli Arabs who live in Israel, Syria, and Lebanon. They speak Arabic and have their own religion and customs. They are famous for making woven carpets and baskets.

Tiberias, on the west coast of Lake Kinneret, has been popular for centuries because of its hot springs, which gush from deep under the ground at 140°F (60°C). People once believed that the warm spring waters could cure many illnesses, but today most visitors come just for a relaxing soak.

If you have time, go and see the local fishermen bringing in their daily catch. The lake is teeming with more than twenty varieties of fish. A great favorite in local restaurants is the St. Peter's fish.

▷ **Vacation time in Galilee** The shores of the Sea of Galilee are popular with Israelis and tourists for relaxing and sightseeing.

▷ **Druze villagers digging up ruins**
In the Galilee region there are many archeological sites, including the ancient Jewish town of Megido.

LIFE IN THE KIBBUTZIM

Israel is well known for its *kibbutzim*. *Kibbutz* is the Hebrew word for a special kind of commune invented by hard-working groups of pioneer Jewish settlers who wanted to live and work together and share everything equally. Deganya Aleph, Israel's oldest kibbutz, was built in 1909 south of the Sea of Galilee. There are now more than 250 kibbutzim all over Israel. They provide Israel with half of its food.

▷ **Kibbutz settlements in Galilee** Each kibbutz includes housing units and a central dining hall and cultural center, along with the modern industry.

▽ **Children at play on a kibbutz** Thanks to warm community life, clean air, and peaceful surroundings, the kibbutzim are ideal places for children.

Agriculture used to be an important part of kibbutz life, but lately industry, including the making of machinery, has become a feature of kibbutz economy.

The people of a kibbutz are called *haverim,* meaning members. The adults meet once a week to discuss matters that concern them all and to take part in votes to accept new members. Children spend all day together in school or special centers and join their families in the afternoon. Haverim eat together in a central dining hall.

Many young people come from abroad every year to spend a few months working on a kibbutz. They can work wherever working hands are needed. But be warned — the work is hard! You can still stay at a kibbutz even if you are not ready for work. Many now have guest houses for tourists.

Haverim have played an important part in the making of modern Israel. They chose to settle in the most difficult places, developed a modern agriculture, and helped defend the country's borders. They have won the respect and praise of many of Israel's great heros. These include Moshe Dayan, an army general (who lost an eye in battle in World War II), and David Ben-Gurion, the first prime minister, or leader, of Israel.

◁ **Harvesting with modern machinery** The best apples are shipped to other countries, and the others are used locally.

19

THE COAST

The Mediterranean coast is where most Israelis live, in and around the lively modern city of Tel Aviv. It is also popular with tourists. Here you can swim, sunbathe, or play a favorite Israeli game of paddle ball, or beach tennis. You will also discover many historic towns and ruins.

Traveling westward in Galilee, you should visit the town of Akko. Its rich and colorful past stretches back 3,500 years. In 1192 the Crusaders made Akko their capital. Crusaders were European Christians who wanted to capture the Holy Land from the Muslims. As you explore the maze of streets, you will find the remains of their city mostly underground. Since the Middle Ages the level of the street has risen by almost 25 feet (8 meters). This is because building has taken place on the sites where houses stood before, a common practice all over Israel.

In the old part of Akko, near the northern city wall, is the marvelous El Jazzar Mosque. It was built in 1781 and is a place of worship for Muslims.

△ **The ruined Roman aqueduct at Caesarea** The aqueduct once carried water from mountain springs to Caesarea. Most of the aqueduct is now buried in the sand.

To the south along the coast road is the city of Haifa (Hefa), today Israel's busiest port and third-largest city. The hill above Haifa is Mount Carmel. Halfway up its steep slope is the Bahai Shrine with its golden dome and beautiful Persian gardens. Instead of walking up the slope, you can take the Carmelit, the only cable-car train in Israel.

At the southern end of Haifa is Mount Carmel National Park, Israel's largest forest reserve. Here, many different birds can be seen as they fly between Africa and Europe.

Farther down the coast you can visit the ruins of the once splendid Caesarea. Named after the Roman ruler Julius Caesar, it was the capital of this region in his time.

△ **Sacred Haifa** Haifa is the center of the Bahai faith, which has three million followers throughout the world. This view of the city is from the Bahai Shrine on Mount Carmel.

◁ **View of Haifa Harbor** In the foreground is the dome of the Bahai Shrine. On the wharf, cranes load goods into cargo ships.

TEL AVIV

About 30 miles (48 kilometers) south of Caesarea along Israel's coastline you will arrive at the modern city of Tel Aviv.

Tel Aviv began in 1909. It started as a neighborhood just outside the ancient city of Jaffa (in Hebrew, Yafo), where the world-famous Jaffa oranges are grown. Tel Aviv was once called "the white town" because all its houses were painted pure white. Today, Tel Aviv is the larger of the two cities, which were officially joined in 1950. It is now known as "the first New Hebrew town," and has a truly international atmosphere. The old crumbling section of Yafo was later restored and is now a popular tourist area.

Tel Aviv is also Israel's main business center. In the Ramat Gan, a small city next to Tel Aviv, the polishing of diamonds is an important industry worth billions of dollars a year. Try to see the amazing exhibits at the Harry Openheimer Diamond Museum. The nearby University Campus, with its museum that helps visitors understand Jewish history, is also worth a visit.

At the Haaretz Museum you can see fascinating archeological and historical findings from the region, including coins, glassware, and ceramics. The fountain in Dizengoff Square is a spectacular landmark in Tel Aviv. Flames shoot up above plumes of water while recorded music plays in the background. To relax, walk by the sea along the Promenade, a favorite place for a stroll.

In Yafo, the Shalom Building, 35 stories high, is a major modern landmark. From its top you have an excellent view of Tel Aviv as well as half the country of Israel. Most of the building is used as offices.

▷ **Tel Aviv Promenade** On the road running parallel to the seashore are hotels, cafés, and restaurants.

▽ **The ancient port of Yafo** In biblical times the cedar trees used to build the Jewish Temple were brought here in ships.

◁ **Old restored Yafo homes** In the ancient city, most of the streets twist and turn and are narrow like this.

MODERN CITIES, OLD TRADITIONS

To the south of Tel Aviv is Ashdod, another busy, modern port city. It has grown quickly in the last thirty years and is now an industrial center where 85,000 people live.

Israelis love to eat, and in cities like Ashdod there is a huge choice of food at restaurants and street stands. *Falafel* — fried, spicy chick-pea balls eaten with pita bread and salad — is the national snack, but

▽ **Street stalls in Jericho** City life, fashion, music, and soft drinks in Israel are similar to those in all western countries.

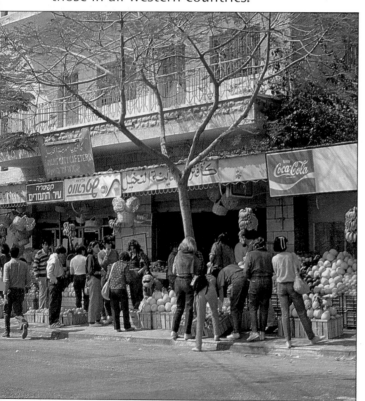

hamburgers, ice cream, and pizzas are just as popular. Israelis also like vegetables and fruits. Watermelons are a special favorite when they are in season.

In the Jewish religion, there are many laws about food. They are known as the *kosher* laws. For example, they forbid the eating of pork. And the meat of animals that are allowed must be be prepared in special ways, such as only well done. The *kosher* laws also forbid the eating of meat and dairy products together.

Since biblical times, the Jewish day of rest — *Shabbat* in Hebrew — is Saturday. Religious Jews are not allowed to do any work on that day, including driving a car, cooking, or writing. But most Israelis are nonreligious, and their favorite popular tradition on weekends is taking sightseeing trips, walks in nature reserves, or picnics. So, on Saturday nights when everyone heads home, the traffic jams resemble rush-hour on a weekday.

Many old traditions live on in Israel. Many Arab men still wear the traditional headdress called the *kaffiyeh*. Most Orthodox Jews dress in black trousers and coat and wear a black hat, or *yarmulke*, a skull cap. Their clothes have a special meaning, reminding them that they are humble before God and must not be vain. Many also grow beards and arrange their hair to have side curls called *payot*.

▷ **Festive meal** A religious Jewish family celebrates Passover, which honors the ancient Israelites' exodus from Egypt.

▽ **A street corner in Tel Aviv** Street names are usually written both in Hebrew and Latin letters.

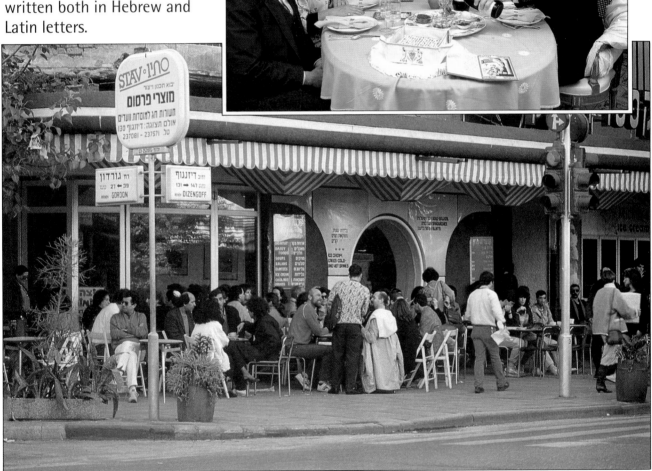

THE DESERT AND THE SEA

The Negev is the large desertlike region in southern Israel. This mostly dry region makes up over half of the country's land area, but only one in ten Israelis lives here. Kibbutzim have had some success in farming this land, and there are a few lush, green places that are like "oases." They stand out from the rest of the barren scenery. To create these oases, water was brought here from the Sea of Galilee.

The region's capital is Beersheba (Be'er Sheva), also known as the "Gateway to the Negev." Because of the heat, people dress differently in the Negev from elsewhere in Israel — you will not see many suits and ties here. Many of Israel's Bedouins lead their traditional way of life in the Negev. They travel to Beersheba to sell their camels, goats, and cloth at the weekly Bedouin market.

▽ **The fun capital of Israel** Elat's warm waters make it ideal for watersports. Windsurfing is a popular activity here.

◁ **Diver's paradise** The clear water of the Gulf of Aqaba and Red Sea are excellent for exploring the coral reefs.

▽ **A vacation village** Along the gulf coast are public and private beaches and many exclusive hotels.

South of Beersheba is the town of Elat (Eilat). This lies on the shores of the Gulf of Elat, also known as the Gulf of Aqaba, an arm of the Red Sea. Fifty years ago only a few hundred people lived in the town. Now Elat has become an important commercial center and a major vacation resort. The oil that Israel buys from other countries is brought ashore here.

The weather in Elat is warm and sunny, even in winter. Israelis and foreign visitors flock to Elat to visit the famous coral reef and to enjoy watersports. Walk along the pier and down a staircase to the Coral World Underwater Observatory where you can view the beautiful tropical fish from a room 16 feet (5 meters) under water. Elat is a wonderful place to relax at the end of your visit to Israel.

ISRAEL FACTS AND FIGURES

People

Israel is the land of Jewish people since ancient times, but it has been their state, or nation, only since 1948.

Recent Jewish immigrants come from two main backgrounds. The Sephardi arrived from Spain and Portugal in the 1400s. The Ashkenazi came from Germany and Eastern Europe in the 20th century. Jews born in Israel are known as Sabras.

Arabs are the largest minority. Most of them are Muslims, but the rest are Christians. The Bedouins and the Druze are the smaller minorities.

Trade and Industry

Israel has few natural resources. Therefore, it has to buy oil for its energy from other countries. Factories manufacture goods to sell abroad, and this trade pays for the materials Israel buys.

Israel produces much of the new medical equipment used in modern hospitals around the world. Examples are surgical lasers and CAT scanners that view the inside of the body. With 1.5 million visitors every year, tourism is also an important industry.

△ **A Jewish boy at the Wailing Wall in Jerusalem** He is celebrating his *bar mitzvah*, a traditional religious ceremony for boys once they have reached the age of 13.

Farming

Despite having a climate that does not favor farming, Israel has a successful agricultural industry. Much of this is due to the systems that farmers have invented to bring water to dry areas. Even parts of the desert have been made to bloom. Israeli farmers manage to produce half the country's food needs as well as enough to sell abroad. Citrus fruits, such as grapefruits and oranges, which are grown along the Mediterranean coast, are the main export crops.

Fishing

On the Mediterranean coast and in the Sea of Galilee, fishing is a local occupation. The fish is mainly sold to restaurants, which serve trout, mullet, and sea bass. There is also commercial fish farming of freshwater fish.

Food

Israel is a mix of different cultures, and Israelis enjoy tasting foods from all over the world: Chinese, Italian, French, Indian, American, or Greek, everything goes.

Popular Israeli foods have their roots in the Middle East and include *shishlik* and *kebab* (meats roasted on a skewer), *hummus* (a chick-pea and sesame seed paste), and *pita* (a thin, flat bread).

Chicken is the most popular meat in Israel, and *shnitsel* (fried thin chicken-breast dipped in egg and bread crumbs) with french fries is a favorite dish.

Special foods are eaten to celebrate various festivals. At the Jewish festival of Hanukkah (Chanukah) *sufganiot* (jelly doughnuts) are popular, and at Purim a sweet pastry known as *hammentashen* is eaten.

Schools

All children in Israel go to school between the ages of five and sixteen years, and many attend high school until they are eighteen years old.

Most children go to a state school, religious or secular. Orthodox Jews send their children to schools where they are taught in Yiddish, a language that is a mixture of ancient German and Hebrew. This is because they consider Hebrew a special language that should not be used in daily speech. There are also colleges known as *yeshivas*, which focus entirely on the teaching of Jewish religious knowledge.

Arab children normally go to their own schools, where lessons are taught in Arabic.

The Media

Most of Israel's many newspapers are published in Hebrew or Arabic. The most popular newspaper is the Hebrew afternoon journal *Yediot Ahronot*, and the most famous morning newspaper is *Ha'aretz*. The Arabs produce six daily and six weekly papers in Arabic.

△ **Industry in southern Israel** This is an aerial view of a water-purifying and salt-extracting industrial complex.

The Israel Broadcasting Authority's TV channel is on the air daily from 6:30 A.M. until 1 A.M. People receive some broadcasts from cable channels and by satellite from neighboring countries. The Broacasting Authority also includes a variety of radio stations.

The Arts

There are many drama companies that perform plays ranging from Shakespeare to the new works that are now being written in Israel. The most well known are the Habimah and Cameri Theaters in Tel Aviv and the Haifa Municipal Theater.

There are museums and art galleries throughout Israel. Most important is the Israel Museum in Jerusalem. Here you can see many paintings and sculptures dating from the 1700s to the present day. Many archeological finds, including some of the Dead Sea Scrolls, and exhibits on Jewish life are here, too.

Israel is also famous for the stained-glass Chagall Windows, designed by artist Marc Chagall. Twelve of these can be seen at the Hadassah Hospital, north of the city of Jerusalem.

Israel has produced many authors including Amos Oz from Kibbutz Hulda, Haim Guri, and Moshe Shamir.

The Israel Festival of Music and Drama is a very popular annual event. It draws on local and international groups of performers. World-famous musicians from Israel include the violinists Yitzhak Perlman and Pinchas Zuckerman and the pianist-conductor Daniel Barenboim.

ISRAEL FACTS AND FIGURES

Religion

Jews have lived in Israel since the time of the Old Testament of the Bible. Judaism is Israel's main faith. Christianity was introduced 2,000 years ago and has many followers. The faith of Islam teaches that Jerusalem is the third most holy place in the world, so Israel is also an important home for many Muslims. The Bahai faith has a major center in Haifa.

Sports

Soccer and basketball are the most popular sports in Israel. Watersports are popular along the coastline and around the Sea of Galilee, as is *matkot*, or beach tennis. Israel also has a ski resort on the northeastern slopes of the Mt. Hermon range.

△ **The Church of the Nativity in Bethlehem** It is thought that this is the exact spot where Jesus was born. The priest is holding a Bible.

Plants

The plant life of Israel is extremely varied. On Mount Meron there are subalpine meadows, while 16 miles (25 kilometers) away there is a papyrus swamp. The southern half of the country is dominated by the Negev Region where only scrub grows naturally. There are 2,500 plant species, 150 of which are found only here.

The Israelis are trying to replant acres of forest that were cut down in previous centuries. There is even an official day, Tu B'shevat in February, when children plant new trees.

Animals

There is also a wide variety of animals in Israel. This has been partly due to the efforts of Israeli conservationists. They were determined to restore to Israel the animals mentioned in the Bible but which had become extinct. Asses, ostriches, and gazelles have been reintroduced. Ibex (wild goat) roam the desert mountain areas. You will also find gecko lizards, viper, and birds such as storks and turtledoves.

Festivals

The many Jewish, Islamic, and Christian festivals in Israel include:
March-April-May **'Id-al-Fitr** A Muslim festival to celebrate the end of their month-long fast
May 14 **Independence Day** Commemorates Israel becoming an independent state in 1948

September-October **Yom Kippur** Jewish holy day. A 25-hour period of fasting with no food, no drink
December 25 **Christmas Day** One of many Christian holidays
December-January **Hanukkah** Jewish holiday to honor the victory of the ancient Jews over the Greek rulers the country

HISTORY

The first settlers in Israel can be traced back 500,000 years. Archeologists have discovered evidence of the earth's first forms of agriculture in Israel.

In about 1800 B.C. Abraham, the founder of the Hebrew nation, received a message from God that he and his people should travel to the land that is now Israel, their Promised Land. In 1250 B.C. Moses and the Hebrews escaped from slavery in Egypt to return to the Promised Land, which then became the Land of Israel.

Israel was repeatedly invaded by empires. Between 63 B.C. and A.D. 324 it was the Romans who ruled the country. In A.D. 640 the Arabs conquered Israel but lost it in 1099 to the Crusaders, who came from Europe.

A small Jewish population always remained in Israel, and Jews emigrated to it constantly over the centuries, to live in their Holy Land. On May 14, 1948, David Ben-Gurion, Israel's first prime minister, declared the country to be independent of foreign control.

However, the following years continued to be marked by wars between Israel and several of its neighboring countries, which threatened its existence.

But in 1977 Israel made peace with Egypt. This marked the way for peace with the Palestinians, made in 1993. The peace treaty promised the Palestinians their own government and self-rule in the Gaza Strip and areas in the West Bank. In late 1995 Israel and Jordan set a path toward peace, which should lead to permanent peace in the area.

LANGUAGE

The two official languages in Israel are Hebrew and Arabic. Hebrew is the national language and Arabic is the language of the Arab minorities. English is taught at school and is widely spoken.

Hebrew is the language in which the Bible was first written, but the Jews who founded the state of Israel modified Hebrew into the spoken language of the nation. Hebrew uses an alphabet that differs from Latin letters and is written from right to left. The Hebrew shown at right is a pronunciation guide.

Useful words and phrases

English	Hebrew
One	eh-HAT
Two	sh-TA-yim
Three	sha-LOSH
Four	AR-bah
Five	ha-MESH
Six	shesh
Seven	SHEV-vah
Eight	sh-MO-neh
Nine	TAY-shah
Ten	Esser
Sunday	YOM ree-SHON
Monday	YOM shay-NEE
Tuesday	YOM shlee-SHEE
Wednesday	YOM reh-vee-EE

Useful words and phrases

English	Hebrew
Thursday	YOM ha-mee-SHEE
Friday	YOM shee-SHEE
Saturday	sha-BAT
Good morning	BO-ker tov
Hello/Good-bye	sha-LOM
Please	be-va-ka-SHA
Thank you	to-DAH
Excuse me	slee-ha
How much?	ka-ma?
yes	ken
no	lo
food	OCH-el
water	MY-im

31

INDEX

Note: Place names in Israel have a long history so are denoted in a variety of ways, for example, Yafo and Jaffa; Hefa and Haifa.

Acknowledgments
Book created for Highlights for Children, Inc.
by Bender Richardson White
Editors: Peter MacDonald and Lionel Bender
Designer: Malcolm Smythe
Art Editor: Ben White
Editorial Assistant: Madeleine Samuel
Picture Researcher: Annabel Ossel
Production: Kim Richardson
Maps produced by Oxford Cartographers, England.
Banknotes from Thomas Cook Currency Services.
Stamps from Stanley Gibbons.

Editorial Consultant: Andrew Gutelle
Israel Consultant: Basmat Even-Zohar, Tel Aviv, Israel
Managing Editor, Highlights New Products: Margie Hayes Richmond

Picture credits
JS = Jamie Simson/DAS Photographs. EU = Eye Ubiquitous/James Davis Worldwide Photographic Travel Library.
Z = Zefa.
t = top, b = bottom, l = left, r = right.
Cover: Z Page 6-7: EU/JDWP. 7t: JS. 7br: JS. 8: Z. 9t: Z. 9b: Z. 10l: JS. 10r: Z. 11: Z. 12-13: JS. 13t: JS. 13b: EU. 14-15t: EU. 14-15b: JS. 15: JS. 16: JS. 17t: JS. 17b: EU. 18: JS. 19r: Z/Moshe Zur. 19b: JS. 20l: Z/Starfoto. 20-21: Z. 21tr: EU. 22b: Z. 23t: JS. 23b: Z. 24, 25t, 25b: Z. 26: EU. 26-27: Z. 27: Z. 28: Eye Ubiquitous/John D. Norman. 29: Z. 30: Eye Ubiquitous/Bruce Adams. Illustration on page 1 by Tom Powers.